D0053292

You talked about your dream.
I want to encourage you to go for it!
red

Rules of the Red Rubber Ball

FIND AND SUSTAIN YOUR LIFE'S WORK

by kevin carroll

Printed in China. For information address
Hyperion, 77 West 66th Street, New York, New York 10023-6298.

Book Design:

Willoughby Design Group, Kansas City, Missouri

Photography:

pages iv, 37 b., 37 e., 42 © Getty Images Inc.
pages 6, 7 © Robert Essel NYC/CORBIS

Illustration:

page 37a. © 2004 Aaron Meschon
page 37c. © 2004 Dan Page c /o theispot.com
page 37d. © 2004 Marci Roth
page 37f. © 2004 Schill/SIS
page 61 © 2004 Keri Smith

Original letterpress by Hammerpress, Kansas City, Missouri

Library of Congress Cataloging-in-Publication Data

ISBN 978-1-933060-02-6

ESPN Books are available for special promotions and premiums.
For details contact Michael Rentas, Manager, Inventory and Premium Sales,
Hyperion, 77 West 66th Street, 11th floor, New York, New York 10023,
or call 212-456-0133.

FIRST EDITION

10 9 8 7 6 5 4

THIS BOOK IS DEDICATED TO

all of the believers, teachers & dreamers,
in my life (and there have been many)
but, especially these:

believers
aunt sandy & uncle bobby, aunt wesie
& uncle walt, uncle donald, donnie, kyle,
norman, mel, snooper, keith (aka gucci man),
kavinanina, & my "editor" joanne gordon

teachers
mom-mom & pop-pop, miss lane & mr. lane,
preston playground, "grin", the usaf, randell
gene, coach mac, joe h., st. joe's, al & scottie,
keith a. jones, "h" white, peter r., tinker,
gina w., ann w. & gordon mackenzie

dreamers
auntie ro-ro
my wife/muse kimberlee grace &
L^2 (designer extraordinaire)

ika

CONTENTS

The master in the ART of living
makes little distinction between his
work and his play, his labor and
his leisure, his mind and his body,
his information and his recreation,
his *love* and his religion.

He hardly knows **which** is **hɔihw**.

He simply pursues his vision of
excellence at whatever he does,
leaving others to decide whether
he is **WORKING** or playing.

To him he's always doing ***both***.

— James Michener

The red rubber ball saved my life.

I was born in Bryn Mawr, Pennsylvania in 1958 to parents who eventually aband*ned their three children. My father left before I was three, and I've only seen my mother a handful of times since I was six.

My brothers and I moved in with our grandparents on a modest street in a wealthy suburb of Philadelphia. There, amid the conflicting worlds of affluence, working class families, and down-and-out drug dealers, Mom-mom and Pop-pop raised us. I was a quiet, scrawny kid,

and for a while,

I felt lost.

Then I discovered...

The playground and its wide-open field became my friend. It was a gathering place. It was a free place.

It was where I discovered sports—

AND THE RED RUBBER BALL THAT FUELED MY DREAMS.

Amid the uncertainty of my childhood, the playground became my sanctuary, a magical environment where my worries, shame and low self-esteem disappeared.

There I discovered my gift of speed. Despite my size I could outrun most other kids, and 

became my ticket onto the field.

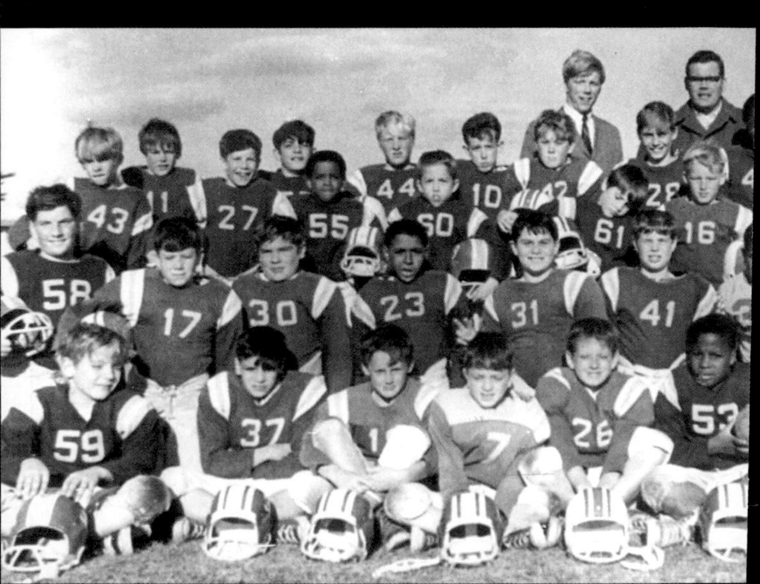

45
22
38
12
19
24
54
34
50
29
51
15

I played whatever sport was in season.

Soccer or football in the

fall; basketball in the winter; baseball or

track in the spring...

I played whatever sport was in season.

Soccer or football in the

fall; basketball in the winter; baseball or

track in the spring...

And the red rubber ball was always there-

A POWERFUL SYMBOL OF SPORT.

For years, I...

chase
ran
caught
kick
kicked
ran
chased

sed
ght
ran
ran
ran
ran
chase
caught
kick

...after that ball.

I was enthralled with whatever sport I played.

I felt ALIVE and POWERFUL.

I felt {loved} and *wanted.*

I grew physically stronger and more confident.

And when recess or playtime was over, when it was time to go inside, I didn't want it to end.

In class I daydreamed about playing in the pros.

{ At night I snuck into a local private school to play on the indoor basketball court. }

)BSESSION OBSESSION OBSESSION OBSESSION OBSE
)BSESSION MY OBSESSION OBSESSION OBSESSION OB
BSESSION OBSESSION OBSESSION OBSESSION OBSES
BSESSION OBSESSION OBSESSION OBSESSION OBSES
BSESSION OBSESSION OBSESSION OBSESSION OBSES
BSESSION OBSESSION OBSESSION OBSESSION OBSES
BSESSION OBSESSION OBSESSION OBSESSION OBSES
BSESSION OBSESSION WITH SPORTS OBSESSION OBS
BSESSION OBSESSION OBSESSION OBSESSION OBSES
BSESSION OBSESSION OBSESSION OBSESSION OBSES
BSESSION OBSESSION OBSESSION OBSESSION OBSES
BSESSION DID NOT GO UNNOTICED, OBSESSION OBSE
BSESSION OBSESSION OBSESSION OBSESSION OBSES
BSESSION OBSESSION OBSESSION OBSESSION OBSES
BSESSION OBSESSION OBSESSION OBSESSION OBSES
BSESSION OBSESSION OBSESSION OBSESSION OBSES

and my elementary school teachers pinned notes to my clothes
for my grandmother to read when I got home.

SESSION OBSESSION OBSESSION OBSESSION OBSES
SESSION OBSESSION OBSESSION OBSESSION OBSE

PLEASE ENCOURAGE
KEVIN TO THINK
ABOUT SOMETHING
OTHER THAN SPORTS.

One time, my grandmother wrote back:

If that's what he loves - so be it!

After my grandmother gave sports her

[STAMP OF APPROVAL],

I knew it was ok to chase that ball.

I was free to play.

I was free to pursue my joy.

SO I DID.

Sports were my passion in the present, and I wanted my passion to be my future. The red rubber ball personified my dream to build a life around sports and became my guiding light,

...a path out of my neighborhood...

...and into the world...

After high school, sports fueled my life choices. I joined the Air Force so I could play soccer in Germany. When I hurt my knee and could no longer play, I studied sports medicine and became an athletic trainer for high school and college teams, and eventually became head trainer for The Philadelphia 76ers, where I was one of the NBA's first black athletic trainers.

My passion for sports also led me to a leadership position at Nike, a company that honors, as well as outfits, athletes.

At Nike, it was my job to inspire. I tried to touch everyone, from shoe designers and marketing staffers to sales teams and retail folks to regional offices and Nike's vendors; it was my job to push their creativity to the limit. I called myself the Katalyst (the 'K' is for Kevin), because I helped spark change. And that is what I still do today as an independent creative consultant who travels around the world working with companies and speaking to people about how sports can change lives, *including my own.*

Even though my jobs have changed over the years, sports have always been connected to my working life. You see, despite the many detours, obstacles and setbacks, I've never lost sight of my red rubber ball. As long as sports were a part of my life in some way—whether I played soccer, treated injured athletes or worked for a company that champions athletes—*I've always been happy and have excelled.*

When my first son was born, I gave him a real red rubber ball with the hope that it would one day take him as far as it had taken me.

I

ask

you...

What's *your* Red Rubber Ball ?!?

Finding your red rubber ball

16052
What's your primal source of joy?

a.

b.

What topics do you love to discuss and ponder?

What dream do you chase?

c.

f.

What would you do for free?

d.

What in life do you find irresistible,
a source of inspiration,
a reason to get out of bed?

What activities enthrall you?

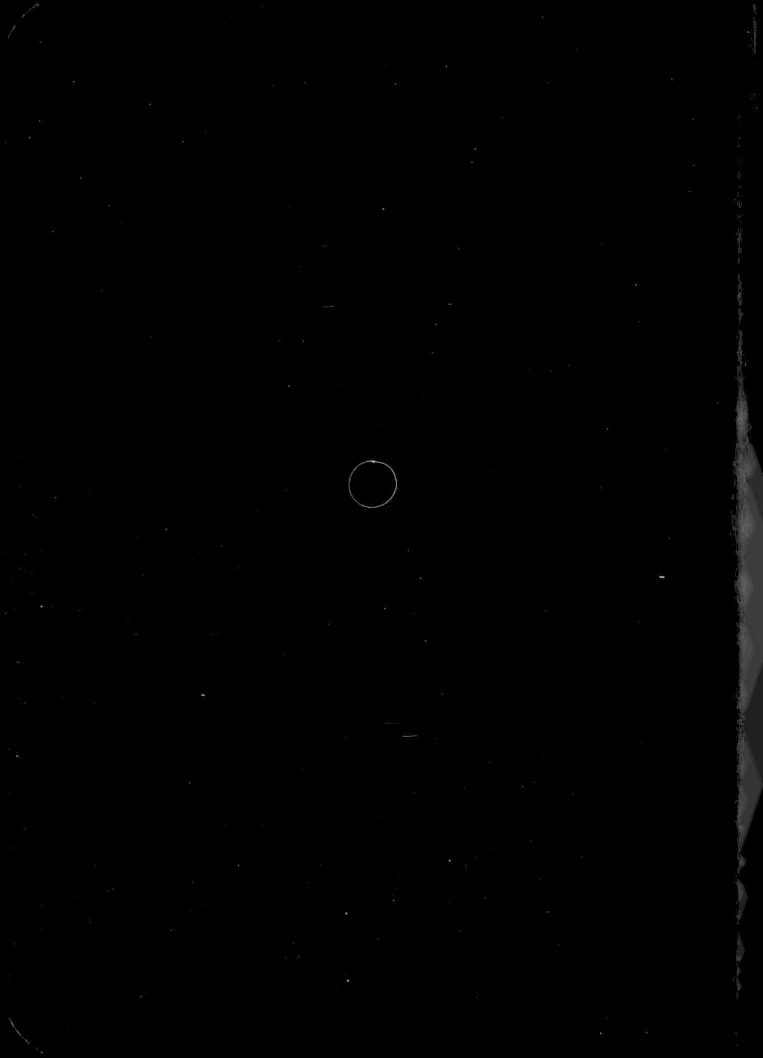

is only
half the battle.

Once you find it, YOU MUST FOLLOW IT,

and that takes

COURAGE,

STRENGTH

and

imagination.

In my own journey, I've discovered guidelines, or rules, that will help ensure you never lose sight of your red rubber ball.

1. Commit to your red rubber ball and it will fuel decisions about what you study, where you work, how you live, whom you befriend, and how you act.

2. Build and nurture relationships, and others will help you pursue your red rubber ball.

3. Be creative, and you'll discover new opportunities.

4. Do the lonely work—those unglamorous tasks that no one asks you to do and that others may never notice—and you will surpass expectations.

5. Speak up and challenge boundaries, and you'll overcome them.

6. Expect and respect the unexpected, and you'll achieve your goals sooner.

7. If you maximize each moment and focus on the present, you'll create the future you desire.

These rules not only kept me on track, but they've resonated with my sons and the thousands of people who have heard me speak publicly over the past five years. I'm honored to share them with you, and hope they serve you well.

Once you find your red rubber ball, may the source of your play become your life's work so much so that no one—*not even you*—will be able to tell the difference between the two.

1

COMMIT TO IT

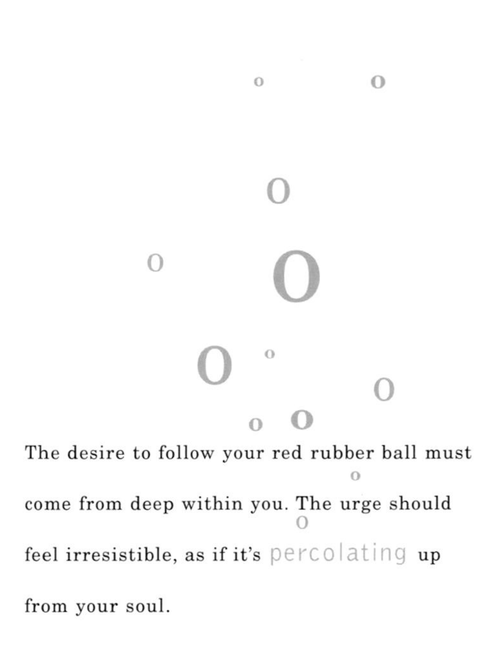

The desire to follow your red rubber ball must come from deep within you. The urge should feel irresistible, as if it's percolating up from your soul.

Desire comes from your *heart,* not from your **HEAD.** It will not always seem like a rational pursuit. It will not always be a path you can justify to others, or yourself.

Doubt is to be expected, *but not obeyed.* Because you will have doubts, and because people will call you "crazy," pursuing your red rubber ball requires real commitment.

It requires commitment to pursue your life's work despite the naysayers; commitment to stick to it in the face of discouragement; and commitment to stay the course despite road blocks.

As a kid people told me,

"Bouncin' that ball will get you nowhere!"

These were the same people who years later asked me for tickets to the Philadelphia 76ers basketball games when I was the team's athletic trainer. If I had listened to the naysayers back then, if I had believed them, or taken what they insisted was a more "appropriate" path for me, then today I would be living someone else's dream and not my own.

Commit to your passion and adversity won't derail you.

2

SEEK OUT ENCOURAGERS

Sustaining your life's work cannot be done

[ALONE]

and you must build relationships with people who have a genuine interest in you and appreciate your commitment to your red rubber ball.

These people are your teachers—

they are your encouragers.

They bless your quest and support you

along the way.

They cheer you on.

They guide you when you lose

your way—*and believe me you will.*

They share your joy when you succeed, and

boost your confidence when you're disheartened.

They help you evaluate options—and they challenge your assumptions.

Most importantly,

THEY GIVE YOU THE COURAGE TO ACT.

When you are with your encouragers, always be present, alert, and on the lookout for teachable moments: that one sentence, story, or nugget of wisdom which will give you the strength to keep pursuing your red rubber ball.

Your teacher may be someone unexpected. Mine was a childhood friend's mother I called Miss Lane.

Miss Lane was with me when my grandmother died and when I left for college. She was there when I joined the Air Force, and after I twisted my knee during a soccer game in Germany and could no longer play sports. Throughout it all she shouldered my sadness and diffused my doubts. She told me over and over again that anything worth having comes with struggle. When I felt lost, she was my confidante and always suggested ways that I might alter my path. When I hesitated taking chances, Miss Lane always fired back:

"Why not?!?"

That's what teachers do, they ask "Why not?"

Still, at the end of the day, I knew that each choice I made was my responsibility, not Miss Lane's.

Do not give your teachers too much power. Their advice is not mandatory, and you do not have to follow it. In the end each decision is yours:

YOU OWN THE OUTCOME, GOOD OR BAD.

Nurture these relationships and treat your teachers well. You'll likely find many along your journey, and together they will constitute a mosaic of mentors who will influence and direct you in untold ways.

influence
Master
1
confidence

3
WORK OUT YOUR CREATIVE MUSCLE

Pursuing your life's work requires CONSTANT CREATIVITY because the paths will not always be obvious or easy to follow.

Sometimes, the paths you want to take will be **BLOCKED** by circumstance or bad luck. The plans you had will

f
a l
l

through.

The people you thought you could count on will let you down.

will help you overcome such unexpected pitfalls.

For creativity to serve you well, you must exercise it daily. You must nourish it, or it will weaken.

HOW?

Break Out of your routine, everyday.

Put yourself in UNCOMFORTABLE situations, everyday.

Look at the world with the innocent eyes of a child by approaching everything in your life with wonder, not assumption.

Be playful, NOT ALWAYS SERIOUS.

To stretch my creative muscle, I dedicate time to an activity that eliminates outside noise and forces me to focus on the moment.

For me, that activity is exercise. I don't work out in a gym—*that's too easy*—instead, I work out in my surroundings, mainly, the city streets where I live in Portland, Oregon. I've created what I call the urban obstacle course, and anything outside—a car, a stoop, a street sign—becomes potential exercise equipment. I hang from light posts to do leg raises; I balance on sidewalk curbs; I jump over fences and cement barricades; do pull ups at bus stop shelters; and use the jungle gym at a local playground for sit ups.

Not surprisingly, I also *solve problems* and get *fresh ideas* when I'm working out. When my body is busy, my mind is *f r e e . . .*

S T R E T C H

your creative muscle, and it will help sustain your life's work.

4

PREPARE TO SHINE

Each day is an opportunity to live out your life's work. There will be quiet moments as well as defining moments, which—if you shine—*will propel you, further than you ever imagined.*

BUT BEWARE. In order to shine in all moments you must prepare. You must do your homework. Preparation means doing what I call *the lonely work*: the unglamorous tasks that no one tells you to do and the hard work that no one will notice.

While studying to be an athletic trainer, I was fanatic about practicing how to tape different size ankles. My kids brought their friends over to the house and I practiced different wrapping techniques on their skinny little ankles. I taped the feet of my friends in the Air Force. I wrapped almost every ankle in my neighborhood. No one told me to do it, and I could have easily reserved all my taping activities for class time. But I knew that the only way I'd get better was through practice.

Meanwhile, in order to pay for school, I also worked full time teaching Czech for the Air Force. I taught class from 11 p.m. until 7 a.m., often letting my students out a bit early so I could catch a nap before my own classes began at eight in the morning. I spent the afternoon working with teams until dinnertime, when I'd go home, do homework and catch another quick nap before reporting back to my evening teaching gig.

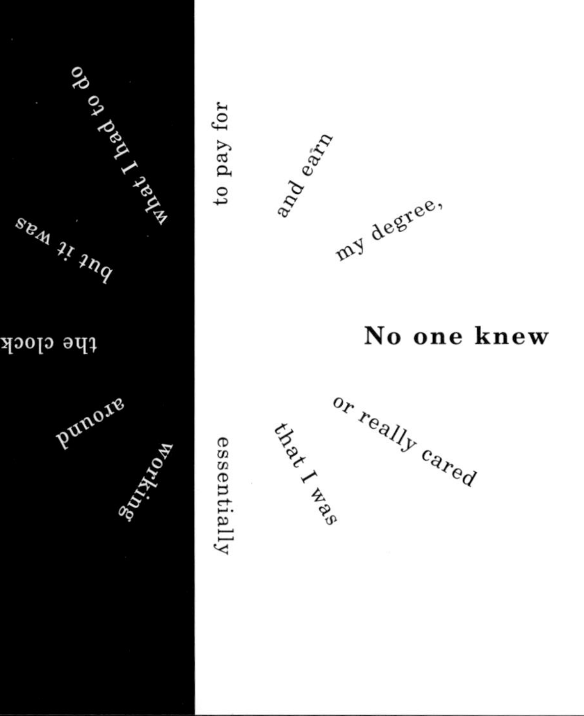
No one knew
or really cared
that I was
essentially
working
around
the clock
but it was
what I had to do
to pay for
and earn
my degree,

Another way to prepare for your shining moments is to study those who have gone before you, and ask questions of people who have more experience than you. Listen to and absorb what worked or failed for them and adopt their most successful tactics and avoid their mistakes.

Pursuing your life's work requires work. The hard work, *the lonely work*, is not always enjoyable, but as long as you do it in the name of your red rubber ball, you will shine.

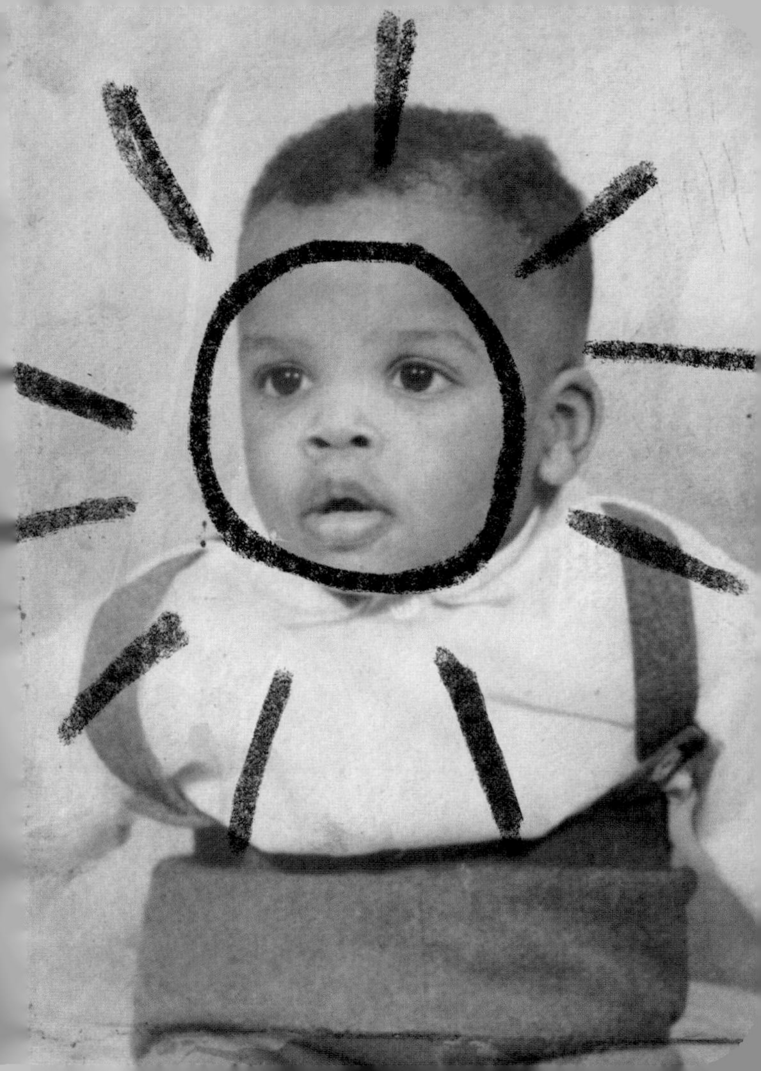

5

SPEAK UP

Never accept the < boundaries > imposed upon you. To truly honor your red rubber ball, you must alter the course when necessary.

Do not recklessly disregard the rules, but do take calculated risks that call upon your knowledge, creativity and courage to say yes when others say no, or no when others say yes.

When I joined the Air Force at age 21, I signed up to join the military police because I thought the M.P. was the quickest way to get out of my neighborhood and to Germany where I could play soccer.

BIG MISTAKE.

I remember the day I sat in a room with dozens of other new recruits to watch a video about our future jobs. The lights dimmed and a video began by showing a single soldier in a huge, puffy parka, holding a M-16 rifle and walking the perimeter of a fence in the deep snow. It was deadly silent and you could actually hear the snow crunching beneath the soldier's feet.

I panicked.
I panicked. I panicked. I panicked. I panicked.
I panicked. I panicked.
I panicked. I panicked.
I panicked.

What had I signed up for? I hated guns and had no intention of spending my future alone, outside in the elements. My mind raced for a solution out of the dismal future I seem to have trapped myself in.

Suddenly, I remembered seeing a small note scribbled on the chalkboard in the next room asking for volunteers for other jobs. The dark room was silent and the most inappropriate thing I could possibly do was disrupt the class. But I was desperate, so I stood up and spoke up:

"Sir, Airman Carroll would like to speak with you!"

An instructor barked back, *"Carroll, what the hell are you doing! Outside now!"*

I held my ground.

"Sir, I don't want this job!"

The instructor lost it, *"What are you talking about Airman? Are you trying to piss me off? Because if you are, you are succeeding!"*

"Sir," I managed, "I saw a note that we could choose to volunteer for another job and I am volunteering!" My heart was pounding.

"Get out of my face, get downstairs and go find out about it," he screamed back.

I had done it!

I had freed myself. I went on to become a language specialist and instructor, a skill that eventually got me assigned to a base in Germany, where the first thing I did was find the local soccer club. In turn, my new skills—I learned five languages including Serbian,

Czechoslovakian, and some Russian—opened up other career doors for me.

I tell that story so you will challenge boundaries when they arise. There's always a way out. You are never trapped as long as you are brave, smart and strategic in your escape. Remember, it's all about honoring your red rubber ball in the face of obstacles.

Sometimes,
to sustain
the quest
for your
red rubber ball, you must speak up.

6

EXPECT THE UNEXPECTED

For all your planning, events will sometimes

unfold in ways you could never have predicted.

But if you expect the unexpected and embrace

it, you will still stay true to your red rubber ball.

One way to {embrace the unexpected} is to be on the lookout for, *and respect,* coincidence. I do not necessarily believe in fate, but, for me, coincidental occurrence strengthens my belief that I'm on the right path.

After the Air Force I returned to Pennsylvania with a degree in sports medicine, and I needed a job. I'd interviewed up and down the East Coast with little luck, but eventually I saw a newspaper ad for a position in an all-boys high school that, *coincidentally,* was located two blocks away from the house where I grew up. It was a very exclusive, "rich boys" school that as a kid I never dreamed of attending. But ironically, there I was, sitting in the athletic director's office interviewing to be the school's athletic trainer and its first black faculty member.

As I sat there, I suddenly realized that the window overlooking the parking lot was the very same window that, as a kid, I had jimmied open from the outside so I could sneak into the school at night and shoot hoops on the basketball court. *How amazing is that!?!*

Some twenty years later there I was, sitting on the other side of the window interviewing for a job. Tickled, I shared the story with the director, and I even showed him how I popped the window's lock! The coincidence was too much for both of us to ignore. He reached into his desk drawer, pulled out a set of keys and tossed them to me.

"Well, you won't need to sneak in here anymore,"

he said.

"You got the job."

I did not take the position at the high school because I once snuck into its gym, but I allowed the coincidence to strengthen my faith that the job was the right choice for me at the time. I embraced it fully, and it eventually led to my next job as an athletic trainer for a college, which led to my position as head trainer for the Philadelphia 76ers, which in turn led to a job at Nike.

The more you prepare and work for your red rubber ball, the more coincidence you will likely encounter. So look out for and have faith in the unexpected twists and turns of life.

7

MAXIMIZE THE DAY

Each day contains 86,400 seconds—that's

86,400 OPPORTUNITIES—to chase,

kick, catch and run after your red rubber ball.

PURSUIT MUST BECOME YOUR DAILY ROUTINE, not a New Year's resolution or a once-a-year sport. It is a constant exercise in listening, learning, preparing and acting.

Begin each day ready to educate yourself. Live each waking moment as if it might be a "teachable moment," *a chance to expand your mind and strengthen your abilities.* End each day feeling confident that you pursued your red rubber ball to the fullest.

There will be days when you'll have difficulty chasing your red rubber ball.

IDLENESS,
low energy,
PERSONAL DISTRACTIONS
lack of confidence
and
NEGATIVE PEOPLE

will all get in your way.

But that's unavoidable. YOU'RE HUMAN. One day off course will not completely derail you. Just don't let those difficult days string together consecutively, or they will turn into weeks, months and years during which you will fail to chase your red rubber ball.

Each day is a chance to re-commit to your red rubber ball. Each day is a chance to find teachers and hear them out. Each day is a chance to look for something unexpected.

Each day offers 86,400 fresh opportunities to work out your creative muscle, to prepare to shine, and to speak up.

Run after your red rubber ball today, and every day it will become your future.

That's it. Simple enough. Seven rules & a red rubber ball.

ENJOY THE CHASE!